2ND EDITION

BEST OF

SUM

MW00575234

ISBN 0-634-06403-7

CORPORATION
7777 W. BLUEMOUND RD. P.O. BOX 13819 MILWAUKEE, WI 53213

In Australia Contact:
Hal Leonard Australia Pty. Ltd.
4 Lentara Court
Cheltenham, Victoria, 3192 Australia
Email: ausadmin@halleonard.com

Visit Hal Leonard Online at
www.halleonard.com

Photo by Emily Sh

CONTENTS

The Bitter End

Words and Music by Deryck Whibley

9

Well,   who   will   greet
Well,   who   will   greet
Well,   who   will   greet

10

All   your   end?

Suy!

18

Fat Lip

Words and Music by Sum 41

1. Storm-ing through the par - ty like my name was El Ni - ño

When I'm

ca - su - al - ty of so - ci - e - ty. I'll nev - er fall_____ in_____ line, be - come an - oth - er

fall in line,

vic - tim of your con - form - i - ty and back down.

down.

down. Down,

Vocal
Chorus
Guitar I
Guitar II
Bass
Drums
A5
E5
C♯5
mi - nor of - fense then. It's none of your con - cern, I guess I'll nev - er learn. I'm sick of be - ing told to wait my
turn. I don't want to waste my time, be - come an - oth - er ca - su - al - ty of so -
waste my time,
E5
B5
C♯m
G♯5
A5
G♯5
I
Pick Scratch

I don't want to waste _____ my _____ time, be-come an-oth-er

waste my time,

ca - su - al - ty of so - ci - e - ty. I'll nev-er fall _____ in _____ line, be-come an-oth-er

fall in line,

Victim of your con - form - i - ty and back down.

40

Heart Attack

Words and Music by Sum 41

42

2. Re-mem-ber when we would hang out ev - 'ry day___

The Hell Song

Words and Music by Sum 41 and Greig Andrew Nori

lieve.   Part of me____ won't a - gree____ 'cause I don't know____ if it's for____

sure.   Sud-den - ly,____   sud-den - ly,____   I don't feel____ so in - se -

68

In Too Deep

Words and Music by Sum 41

1. The fast - er we're fall - in', we're stop - pin' and stall - in'. We're

run - nin' in cir - cles a - gain. Just as things were look - in' up, you said it

74

'Cause I'm in too deep, and I'm try'n' to keep up a-bove in my head in-stead of go-in' un-der. 'Cause I'm in too deep and I'm try'n'

76

2. Seems like each time ____ I'm with you,

I lose my mind ____ be - cause I'm bend - ing o - ver back - wards to re - late. It's

Mr. Amsterdam

Words and Music by Sum 41 and Greig Andrew Nori

[Tuning : Half Step Down]

92

94

no mat-ter how hard I try, _____ I

can't help be bored _____ while this world pass - es by. _____

I can't fight the an-ger, here's a res - ig - na - tion from me, a res - ig - na - tion from

me, a res - ig - na - tion from me, a res - ig - na - tion from

me,   a res - ig - na - tion from me.

Motivation

Words and Music by Sum 41

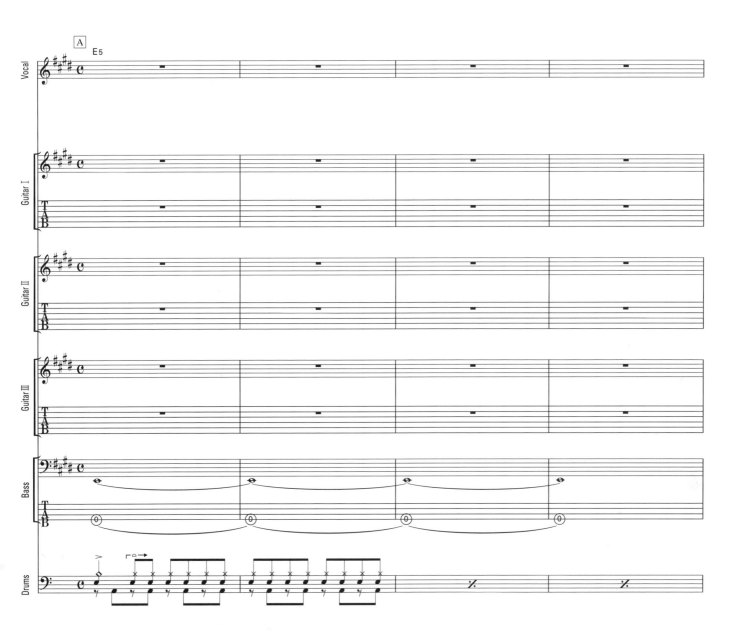

mat - ter what you say,　　　noth-ing's gon - na change my mind.

trend and though I can't pre - tend a friend would be this way, it's not the same but who's to blame for

all those stu - pid things I nev - er said?

114

Vocal lyrics:
Ac - cu - sa - tions, don't know how to take them. In - spi - ra - tion's get - ting hard to fake it.

Con - cen - tra - tion... Sit - u - a - tion nev - er what you want it to be.

No Brains

Words and Music by Sum 41 and Greig Andrew Nori

had e nough___ frus tra - tion.___ I won't get stuck. Good-

- bye. This dead end sit - u - a - tion.___ It's just not worth my

130

134

No Reason

Words and Music by Deryck Whibley and Greig Nori

 Hey! Hey! Hey! Let's go!

How can we   fake this   an - y - more?
(If) noth - ing could   ev - er   be   this   real.

147

Over My Head (Better Off Dead)

Words and Music by Sum 41 and Greig Andrew Nori

152

154

No one plans _____ for it to blow up in their face. _____

Pain for Pleasure

Words and Music by Sum 41

killin' spree through eternity, the devil stabs you in the back.

It's midnight now, you must escape somehow.

170

Pieces

Words and Music by Deryck Whibley and Greig Nori

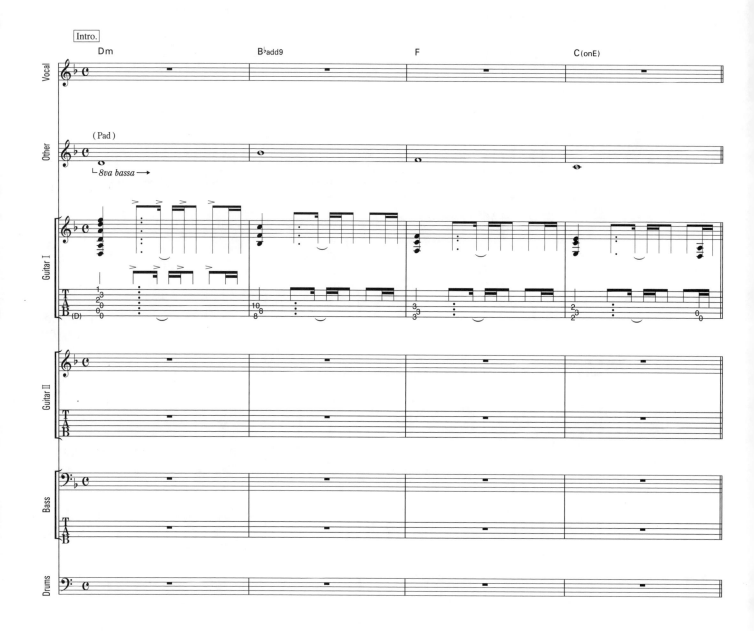

This place is so emp - ty, my thoughts are so tempt - ing. I don't know how___

178

that I'm bet - ter off___ on my___ own.

Still Waiting

Words and Music by Sum 41 and Greig Andrew Nori

Can't find a good rea - son, can't find hope to be - lieve in. _____

1. Drop   dead,   a   bul - let   to   my ___ head.   Your   words   are   like   a

188

198

We're All to Blame

Words and Music by Deryck Whibley, Greig Nori, Steve Jocz and Ben Cook

How can we still suc - ceed tak - ing what we don't need?
Re - al - ize we spend our lives liv - ing in a cul - ture of fear.

Tell - ing lies al - i - bis, sell - ing all the hate that we
Stand to sa - lute and say thanks to the man of the

Welcome to Hell

Words and Music by Deryck Whibley

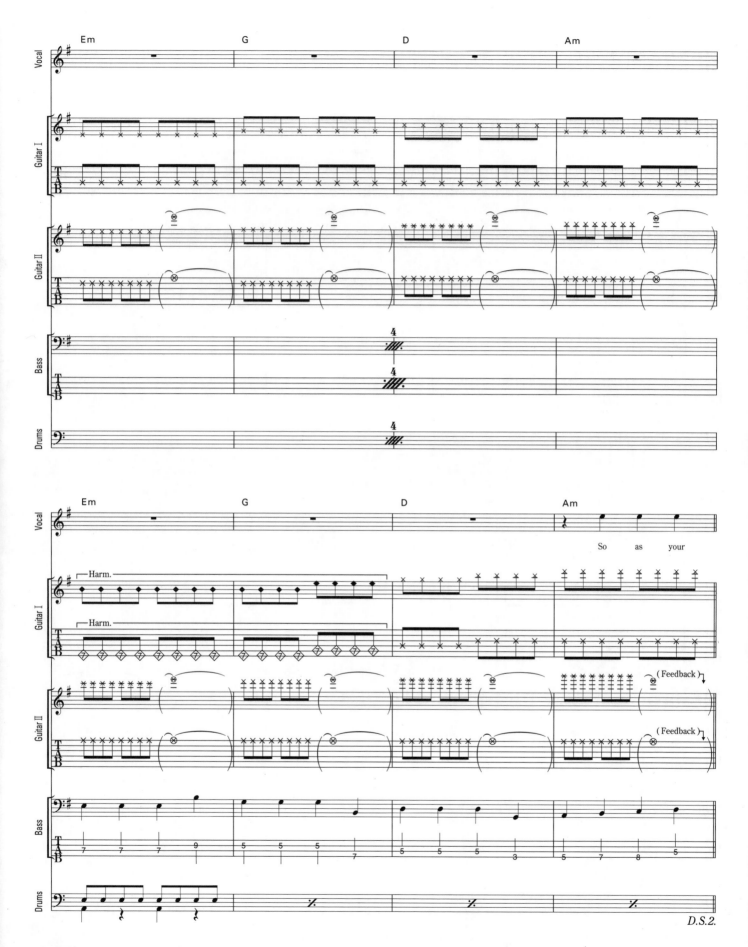

So   as   your

D.S.2.